Searchlight BOOKS™

Understanding the Coronavirus

Heroes of the Pandemic

Margaret J. Goldstein

Lerner Publications ◆ Minneapolis

Lerner Publications Company
An imprint of Lerner Publishing Group, Inc.
241 First Avenue North
Minneapolis, MN 55401 USA

For reading levels and more information, look up this title
at www.lernerbooks.com.

Main body text set in Adrianna Regular.
Typeface provided by Chank.

Library of Congress Cataloging-in-Publication Data

Names: Goldstein, Margaret J. author.
Title: Heroes of the pandemic / Margaret J. Goldstein.
Description: Minneapolis, MN : Lerner Publications, [2022] | Series: Searchlight books : understanding the coronavirus | Includes bibliographical references and index. | Audience: Ages 8–11 | Audience: Grades 4–6 | Summary: "Discover how everyday people became heroes during the COVID-19 pandemic. From medical workers fighting on the frontlines to farmers growing fresh food, readers will uncover how people helped one another during a global health crisis"— Provided by publisher.
Identifiers: LCCN 2020047236 (print) | LCCN 2020047237 (ebook) | ISBN 9781728428475 (library binding) | ISBN 9781728431475 (paperback) | ISBN 9781728430720 (ebook)
Subjects: LCSH: COVID-19 (Disease)—Social aspects—Juvenile literature. | Heroes—Juvenile literature.
Classification: LCC RA644.C67 G647 2022 (print) | LCC RA644.C67 (ebook) | DDC 362.1962/414—dc23

LC record available at https://lccn.loc.gov/2020047236
LC ebook record available at https://lccn.loc.gov/2020047237

Manufactured in the United States of America
1-49384-49488-4/26/2021

Table of Contents

CHAPTER 1

COVID FRONT LINES

In 2020, millions of everyday people became heroes. A new type of virus, known as a novel coronavirus, spread from China around the globe. It causes the disease COVID-19, which gives people coughs, fevers, and aches. The disease sometimes kills people. Since the virus spreads from person to person, many people began working from home to avoid contact with others. But that wasn't possible for everyone. Their workplaces became the front lines of the battle against the disease.

The Strain on Workers

Raymond Lopez worked in a supermarket in Los Angeles, California. He had to work in the store, despite the risk of catching COVID-19. Lopez and his coworkers wore face masks, practiced social distancing, and washed their hands frequently. This limited their risk of catching the virus and spreading it to others.

Essential businesses, such as grocery stores, remained open during the pandemic.

It was a stressful time for Lopez and his coworkers. Customers sometimes ignored the store's safety guidelines. But Lopez remained calm. "It's definitely an atmosphere where everybody's nerves are heightened," he said. "But we don't have time to sit and panic. We have a job to do."

Grocery workers clean and sanitize often to kill the virus on surfaces. Researchers found that the virus can live up to twenty-four hours on certain surfaces.

STEM Spotlight

A virus is a tiny particle that infects living cells and can cause disease. The virus that causes COVID-19 is a coronavirus. *Coronavirus* means "crown virus." Each virus particle is covered by spikes like points on a crown.

Once the virus enters the human body, its spikes fit into notches in cells like keys fitting into locks. The virus enters the cells and begins to reproduce. It makes thousands of copies of itself. This infection makes the person sick.

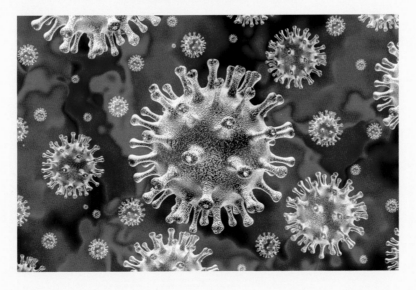

Chapter 2

HEALTH CARE HEROES

As people became sick with COVID-19, health professionals fought the disease. Hospitals filled up with COVID-19 patients. New York City became a COVID-19 hot spot and needed help. In April 2020, doctors, nurses, and physician's assistants from dozens of US states traveled there to help care for COVID-19 patients. They tested patients' hearts and lungs. They administered medicines. They hooked up oxygen masks and ventilators for patients who had trouble breathing.

In Harm's Way

When caring for COVID-19 patients, doctors, and nurses had to make sure they didn't get sick too. Since the virus travels through the air, health professionals protected their skin with gowns and gloves. They wore face masks and face shields to keep the virus from entering their mouths and noses.

New York City was hit hard by the pandemic. Some doctors and nurses worked in a temporary field hospital in Central Park.

Dr. Anthony Fauci

As COVID-19 spread across the United States, many Americans looked to Dr. Anthony Fauci (*below*) for guidance. He is the director of the National Institute of Allergy and Infectious Diseases, a US government agency. COVID-19 and other infectious diseases develop when germs enter the body. Fauci is an expert on these diseases. He has helped control outbreaks of HIV, Ebola, and other deadly infections. In January 2020, Fauci joined the White House Coronavirus Task Force. He also serves as chief medical advisor to US president Joe Biden.

Paramedics were also on the front lines. They treated medical emergencies and rushed sick people to the hospital. They also wore protective gear.

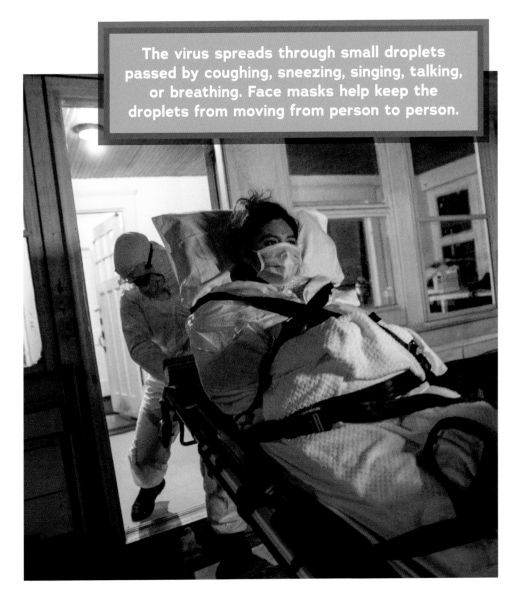

The virus spreads through small droplets passed by coughing, sneezing, singing, talking, or breathing. Face masks help keep the droplets from moving from person to person.

Some people who got sick had to be rushed to the hospital in ambulances. Others recovered at home.

A lot of health workers feared catching the virus from their patients. Kylie Harmon, a paramedic from Texas, tried to stay strong. "I want to help people, even if that's putting myself at risk," Harmon said. "That's something I'm willing to do."

Health workers helped patients who had trouble breathing.

Chapter 3

HANDS TO WORK

As the virus spread, some hospitals ran out of personal protective equipment (PPE). Some health workers reused medical masks or used bandanas as masks. Some even wore trash bags instead of medical gowns. Without proper protection, doctors and nurses were at extra risk of catching COVID-19.

THE PANDEMIC REVEALED THAT THE US HAD A SEVERE SHORTAGE OF PPE.

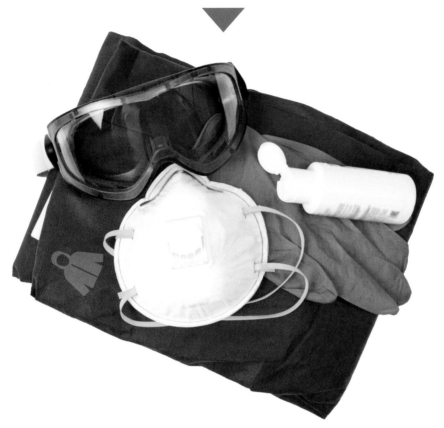

People all over the United States wanted to help. Some sewed masks for health care workers. Others sewed gowns. Americans donated thousands of masks and other protective gear to hospitals so that health care heroes could focus on their work.

People helped in other ways. A group called Unidos en Salud gave free COVID-19 tests in San Francisco, California. By the end of 2020, the group had tested more than 14,000 people. If a person tested positive, volunteers told them to go into quarantine. Volunteers also helped those with COVID-19 find medical care.

In the US, thousands of people were tested for COVID-19 each day.

People protected themselves from the virus by wearing masks and using hand sanitizer.

The Show Must Go On

Not all COVID-19 heroes worked on health care projects. Some volunteered to be poll workers during the 2020 US elections. In the past, many poll workers were over the age of sixty. The virus is especially dangerous for older people, so many seniors did not want to work in crowded polling places. Younger people stepped up and worked the polls so that their neighbors could cast ballots.

Over sixty-five million people voted by mail-in ballots in the 2020 US presidential election.

Many Americans voted by mail rather than going to polling places. Mail carriers delivered millions of ballots to voters and made sure that completed ballots reached election offices.

Shaivi Shah

COVID-19 is especially hard for people without homes. They cannot keep a social distance. They don't have easy access to bathrooms for handwashing. Fifteen-year-old Shaivi Shah of Los Angeles, California wanted to help. In March 2020, she launched a GoFundMe campaign. She used the money to make COVID-19 safety kits for the homeless. The kits contained soap, hand sanitizer, and face masks. By February 2021, Shavi had donated more than 4,600 kits to homeless shelters and food pantries across Southern California.

Beyond the election, mail carriers delivered medical prescriptions and other essential goods so that people could stay safely at home. Delivery drivers were also heroes. They carried groceries and other goods from stores to homes. Millions more stayed on the job during the pandemic. Bus drivers made sure that essential workers got to their jobs each day. Teachers taught kids online and in classrooms. Other workers kept the nation's food supply strong. They picked fruits and vegetables on farms and staffed food-processing plants.

Most Americans avoided stores during the pandemic. They ordered items for home delivery instead.

Chapter 4

LOOKING FORWARD

The world needed a long-term solution to control the virus. Scientists got to work on a vaccine. Thousands of people volunteered to take part in vaccine trials. These heroes risked unknown side effects from the unproven vaccines, but they wanted to help. "Participating in a vaccine trial is really empowering," said volunteer Stella Sexton. "You feel like you are taking action and doing something to help solve the crisis."

In November 2020, two drug companies, Pfizer and Moderna, announced that they had developed effective COVID-19 vaccines. The companies began plans to make millions of vaccine doses to protect people around the world. The World Health Organization, Centers for Disease Control and Prevention, and other organizations worked to decide which groups of people should get first access to the vaccine.

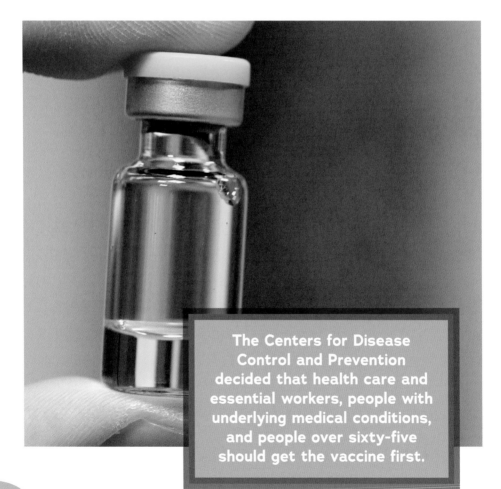

The Centers for Disease Control and Prevention decided that health care and essential workers, people with underlying medical conditions, and people over sixty-five should get the vaccine first.

MOST VACCINES ARE ADMINISTERED BY INJECTION WITH A NEEDLE.

▼

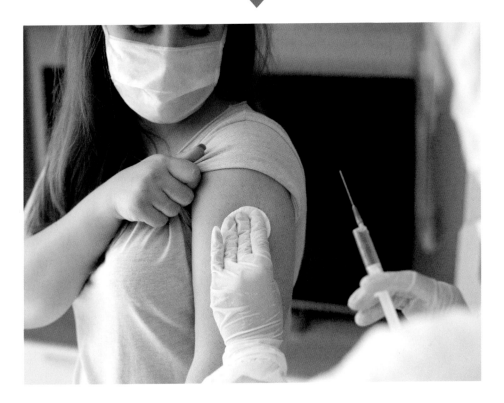

While health workers made plans to distribute vaccines, medical researchers looked for medicines to treat COVID-19. Certain drugs helped some patients but not others. Others didn't work at all, or they made patients even sicker. Researchers kept digging for a treatment.

STEM Spotlight

A vaccine prepares your body to fight an invader, such as a virus. The COVID-19 vaccine is made using brand-new technology. The vaccine contains a substance called messenger RNA. It triggers cells to make a type of protein found in COVID-19. The protein is harmless, but your immune system thinks it's COVID-19 and gets ready to fight the virus. Later, if COVID-19 does enter your body, your immune system will have its defenses ready, so you won't get sick.

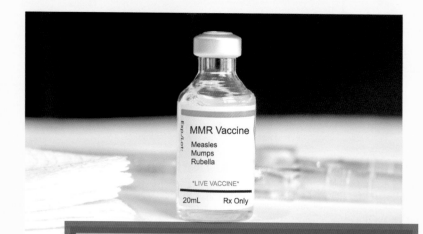

The COVID-19 vaccine looks similar to other common vaccines. However, the way it works inside the body is different.

HERD IMMUNITY

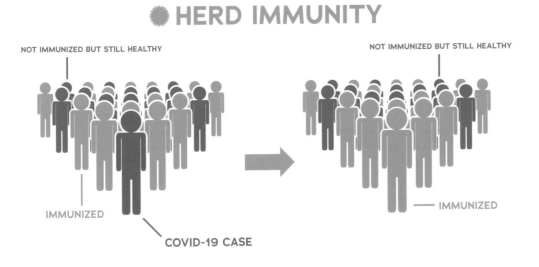

NOT IMMUNIZED BUT STILL HEALTHY

NOT IMMUNIZED BUT STILL HEALTHY

IMMUNIZED

COVID-19 CASE

IMMUNIZED

NOT IMMUNIZED

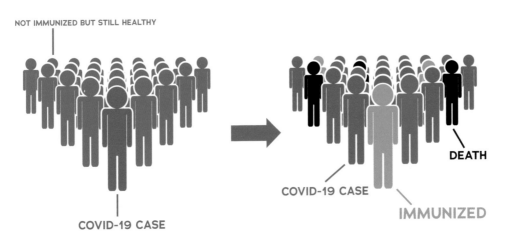

NOT IMMUNIZED BUT STILL HEALTHY

COVID-19 CASE

COVID-19 CASE

DEATH

IMMUNIZED

The more people who get the vaccine, the less the virus can spread. Herd immunity is achieved when a high percentage of the population is vaccinated and has immunity.

Governments also played a big role. State and local health agencies made rules to keep people safe. They kept track of how many people were infected and how many got sick. They taught citizens the importance of social distancing, washing hands, and wearing masks.

Most businesses and public places required people to wear face coverings except for when eating or drinking.

Face masks must be worn

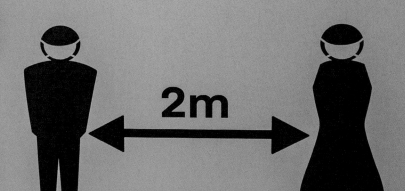

FOR OUR HEALTH PLEASE WEAR A MASK AND PRACTICE SOCIAL DISTANCING

2m

KEEP A SAFE DISTANCE

Experts recommended standing at least 6 feet (2 m) away from others to reduce the spread of COVID-19.

Staying home as much as possible was the best way to keep the virus from spreading and protect frontline heroes.

Everyone had a part to play—from doctors to grocery workers. They worked together and followed the advice of scientists. These COVID-19 heroes worked hard to keep everyone safe.

Important Dates

December 2019   Government officials in China report a new virus outbreak in the city of Wuhan.

January 2020   Health officials report the first COVID-19 case in the United States.

February 2020   The World Health Organization names the disease caused by the virus COVID-19, which stands for "coronavirus disease 2019." A patient in Santa Clara County, California, is the first person in the United States known to die from COVID-19.

April 2020   In New York state, about 200,000 people are diagnosed with COVID-19.

August 2020   More than 20 million people worldwide have tested positive for COVID-19.

October 2020   US president Donald Trump gets sick with COVID-19. He was taken to a hospital where he recovered.

November 2020   The drug companies Pfizer and Moderna announce the development of effective COVID-19 vaccines.

Glossary

cells: basic structures found in all living things

coronavirus: a virus whose surface is covered by spiky projections

essential worker: a person whose work is needed to keep society running

immunity: the ability to resist a certain disease

infection: a disease or sickness caused by germs

pandemic: a worldwide outbreak of a disease

positive: having an infection or illness, as indicated by a test result

quarantine: a specific time period during which people isolate themselves from others so as not to pass on a disease

social distancing: keeping a certain amount of space between yourself and others, usually 6 feet (2 m), to prevent the spread of disease from person to person

vaccine: a substance that prepares the immune system to fight off an invader, such as a virus

ventilator: a device that pushes air into a person's lungs to keep them breathing normally

virus: a tiny particle that can infect living cells and cause disease

Learn More

Facts about Coronavirus
   https://kids.nationalgeographic.com/science/article/facts-about
   -coronavirus

Farndon, John. *Plague: Epidemics and Scourges through the Ages*.
   Minneapolis: Lerner Publications, 2017.

The Ultimate Kids' Guide to the New Coronavirus
   https://www.livescience.com/coronavirus-kids-guide.html

UTHSC Coronavirus Facts for Kids
   https://uthsc.edu/coronavirus/documents/coronavirus-kids-fact-sheet.pdf

Williams, Heather DiLorenzo. *Essential Workers, Essential Heroes*.
   Minneapolis: Lerner Publications, 2020.

Williams, Heather DiLorenzo. *Social Distancing*. Minneapolis: Lerner
   Publications, 2020.

Index

Photo Acknowledgments

Image credits: FG Trade/Getty Images, p. 5; Ulet Ifansasti/Getty Images, p. 6; Lightspring/Shutterstock, p. 7; Spencer Platt/Getty Images, p. 9; Tasos Katopodis/Getty Images, p. 10; John Moore/Getty Images, p. 11; OgnjenO/Getty Images, p. 12; Morsa Images/Getty Images, p. 13; StanislauV/Shutterstock, p. 15; zstock/Shutterstock, p. 16; Megan Varner/Getty Images, p. 17; Octavio Jones/Getty Images, p. 18; Nopphon_1987/Shutterstock, p. 19; Stephanie Keith/Getty Images, p. 20; Hendrik Schmidt-Pool/Getty Images, p. 22; Studio Peace/Shutterstock, p. 23; SamaraHeisz5/Shutterstock, p. 24; Miloje/Shutterstock, p. 25; Catherine McQueen/Getty Images, p. 26; mixetto/Getty Images, p. 27; Aaron of L.A. Photography/Shutterstock, p. 28

Cover: adamkaz/Getty Images